MW00377745

THIS BOOK BELONGS TO:

She Believed She Could Journal

36123977R00062

Made in the USA
San Bernardino, CA
18 May 2019